NICK FAWCETT

GOD BLESS YOU

Prayers of Blessing and Consecration
for All Occasions

GOD BLESS YOU
Prayers of Blessing and Consecration for All Occasions

Copyright © 2005 Nick Fawcett.
Original edition published in English under the title
GOD BLESS YOU by Kevin Mayhew Ltd, Buxhall,
England.

This edition copyright © Fortress Press 2019

All rights reserved. Except for brief quotations in critical articles or reviews, no part of this book may be reproduced in any manner without prior written permission from the publisher. Email copyright@augsburgfortress.org or write to Permissions, Fortress Press, PO Box 1209, Minneapolis, MN 55440-1209.

Cover image: Cover art by Studio-Pro from iStock
Cover design: Alisha Lofgren

Print ISBN: 978-1-5064-5922-6

GOD BLESS YOU

Prayers of Blessing and Consecration for All Occasions

Nick Fawcett

Contents

Introduction	10

People

The local church family

1	Blessing of a new Christian	11
2	Confirmation blessing/ blessing of a new church member	12
3	Blessing of a candidate for believer's baptism	12
4	Blessing of youth workers/Sunday school staff	13
5	Blessing of a pastoral team	14
6	Blessing of a healing team	14
7	Blessing of church cleaners	15
8	Blessing of a catering team	15
9	Blessing of a new vicar	16
10	Blessing of a new curate	16
11	Blessing of a new ordinand/trainee minister	17
12	Blessing of a vicar leaving for a new parish	18
13	Blessing of lay readers/deacons/ elders/church wardens	18
14	Blessing of a church choir/choristers	19
15	Blessing of a church music group	20

The wider Church

16	Commissioning of a new missionary	20
17	Commissioning of an industrial chaplain	21
18	Commissioning of a hospital chaplain	21
19	Commissioning of a hospice chaplain	22
20	Commissioning of an armed forces chaplain	22
21	Commissioning of a university/college chaplain	23

The wider world

22	Blessing of a newly conceived child	24
23	Blessing of a miscarried child	24
24	Blessing of a stillborn child	25
25	Blessing of a newborn child	26
26	Blessing of a premature child	26
27	Blessing of a mentally disabled child	27
28	Blessing of a physically disabled child	27

29	Blessing of a child with learning difficulties	28
30	Blessing of a child starting school	28
31	Blessing of a young person before an examination	29
32	Blessing of a son or daughter leaving home	29
33	Blessing of parents/a parent when a daughter or son leaves home	30
34	Blessing of a first-year university/college student	30
35	Blessing of someone starting a new job	31
36	Blessing of someone on *her*/*his* retirement	32
37	Blessing of a new home	33
38	Blessing of a person or family moving away	33
39	Blessing of an engagement ring	34
40	Blessing of a couple on the start of completion of premarital counseling	34
41	A wedding blessing—for bride and groom (1)	35
42	A wedding blessing—for bride and groom (2)	35
43	Blessing of a new parent	36
44	Blessing on the renewal of wedding vows	36
45	Blessing of replacement wedding rings	37
46	Blessing at a silver, ruby, golden, or diamond wedding celebration	37
47	Blessing of the elderly	38
48	Blessing of the sick	38
49	Blessing before an operation	38
50	Blessing of an AIDS sufferer	39
51	Blessing of an Alzheimer's sufferer	40
52	Blessing of the terminally ill	40
53	Blessing of the dying	41
54	Blessing for the victim of a sudden or violent death	42
55	A funeral blessing—for the deceased	42
56	A funeral service—at close of service	43
57	A graveside blessing	43
58	A cremation blessing	44
59	Blessing during the interment of ashes	44
60	Blessing during the scattering of ashes	45

Society

61	Blessing for the police	45
62	Blessing for firefighters	46
63	Blessing for ambulance staff and paramedics	46
64	Blessing for a GP	47

65	Blessing for a nurse	48
66	Blessing for a caregiver	48
67	Blessing for members of the armed forces	49
68	Blessing for fishermen	50
69	Blessing for a farm/farmers	50
70	Blessing for teachers	51
71	Blessing for shop workers	51
72	Blessing for factory workers	52
73	Blessing for office workers	53
74	Blessing for a school assembly	54

Buildings

Church-related

75	Consecration of a church sanctuary	55
76	Consecration of a church hall	56
77	Consecration of Sunday school facilities	56
78	Consecration of day care facilities	57
79	Consecration of a church extension	58
80	Consecration of a church vestibule	58
81	Consecration of a church kitchen	59
82	Consecration of a church office	60
83	Consecration of a local ecumenical project	60
84	Consecration of an interfaith center	61

In the wider world

85	Consecration of a school/classroom	62
86	Consecration of a hospital/hospital ward	62
87	Consecration of a nursing/residential care home	63
88	Consecration of a psychiatric hospital/ward	64
89	Consecration of a hospice	64
90	Consecration of a homeless shelter	65
91	Consecration of a prison	66
92	Consecration of a new small business	66
93	Consecration of a supermarket	67
94	Consecration of a factory	68
95	Consecration of an office	69

Church Fittings and Furnishings

| 96 | Consecration of a cross | 70 |
| 97 | Consecration of an organ/piano/keyboard | 71 |

98	Consecration of chairs/pews	72
99	Consecration of a stained-glass window	72
100	Consecration of a memorial plaque	73
101	Consecration of an altar/communion table	74
102	Consecration of a banner	74
103	Consecration of kneelers	75
104	Consecration of a font	76
105	Consecration of a baptismal pool	76
106	Consecration of a chalice	77
107	Consecration of a communion plate	78
108	Consecration of facilities for the disabled	78
109	Consecration of bells/bell-ropes	79
110	Consecration of a church notice board	80
111	Consecration of a church Bible	80
112	Consecration of hymn books	81
113	Consecration of prayer books	82
114	Consecration of a church library	82
115	Consecration of an amplification/public address system	83
116	Consecration of an audio-visual system	84
117	Consecration of a church clock	84
118	Consecration of a church passenger vehicle	85

Church Events

119	Blessing of a multi-church event	86
120	Blessing of an interfaith project/event	86
121	Blessing of a public expression of faith	87
122	Blessing of an outreach service/event	88
123	Blessing of a harvest supper	88
124	Blessing of a church meal/event to fight hunger	89
125	Blessing of a church lunch	90
126	Blessing of a church fundraiser	90
127	Blessing of a craft exhibit	91
128	Blessing of a flower festival	92
129	Blessing of a church concert	92
130	Blessing of a youth group event	93
131	Blessing of a quiet day or retreat	94
132	Blessing of a church anniversary	94
133	Blessing of a church outing	95
134	Blessing of a church weekend	96

135	Blessing of a church/council meeting	96
136	Blessing of a new house group/study group	97

The Lord's Supper

137	Blessing of bread (1)	98
138	Blessing of bread (2)	98
139	Blessing of bread (3)	99
140	Blessing of bread (4)	99
141	Blessing of wine (1)	100
142	Blessing of wine (2)	100
143	Blessing of wine (3)	101
144	Blessing of wine (4)	101

Money

145	Blessing of a weekly offering (1)	102
146	Blessing of a weekly offering (2)	102
147	Blessing of a weekly offering (3)	103
148	Blessing of a weekly offering (4)	103
149	Blessing of a weekly offering (5)	104
150	Consecration of a collection for charity	104
151	Consecration of proceeds from a fundraising event	105
152	Consecration of a gift	105
153	Consecration of a legacy	106

Places

154	Consecration/re-consecration of a cemetery/graveyard	107
155	Consecration/re-consecration of a crematorium	108
156	Dedication of a garden of remembrance	108
157	Dedication of a tree planted in memory of a loved one	109

Animals

158	Blessing of a new family pet	110
159	Blessing when a pet has to be put down	111
160	Blessing at the burial of a family pet	111
161	Blessing of an animal sanctuary	112

*To Colin and Jude Randall,
in appreciation of your ministry and friendship*

Introduction

It was an unusual request: a prayer for the blessing of new bell-ropes—hardly a topic that naturally springs to mind! For a moment I was uncertain, not just about what to pray for but equally about the whole concept of blessing, for what does it say about God? Are we suggesting his approval and favor hinges upon a few words of consecration? Surely not. The rationale behind such prayers lies elsewhere, stemming from our instinctive desire to entrust ourselves, our loved ones, and our world into God's gracious keeping. We want to express our care, concern, and commitment. We yearn to make a difference to the community in which we live. We need to articulate our faith in God's purpose and our dependence on his love. And yes, we believe that prayer somehow makes a difference, not determining what God does but contributing to the fulfillment of his will.

For clergy, chaplains, and those with pastoral responsibility, requests to conduct blessings are surprisingly frequent. During my own time in ministry, among the many items I was asked to consecrate were hymn books, chairs, banners, memorial plaques, a cross, and an electronic piano, not to mention a church lounge, amplification system, hi-fi, and tent! Then, of course, there were blessings at births and baptisms, weddings and funerals, together with those at hospitals, nursing homes, social events, church fairs, shared meals, and the Lord's Supper. And so I could go on. No book can cover every contingency, but I have tried here to provide a resource covering a broad spectrum of life—both within the church and further afield—the choice of subjects reflecting the conviction that God is as much involved in the secular as the "sacred," in the everyday world of work as the Sunday world of worship.

It is my hope and prayer that something of this book may prove a blessing to you and to others.

NICK FAWCETT

People

The local church family

1
Blessing of a new Christian

May Christ who has touched your heart
    and captured your imagination
    richly bless you in all that lies ahead.
May he be a constant source of joy and strength,
    supporting, sustaining,
    equipping, and enabling,
    a daily companion as you walk his way.
Whatever life may bring,
    the Lord surround you with love,
    encircle you with peace,
    and fill you with hope
    until the journey is over,
    the race run,
    and you meet him face to face,
    celebrating his goodness forevermore.
Amen.

2
Confirmation blessing/blessing of a new church member

May the living Christ bless you
    through the fellowship of his people,
    granting you, as a member of his body,
    support, encouragement, guidance, and inspiration.
May you give and receive,
    love and be loved,
    actively contributing to the life and witness
    of this church
    through the service you offer,
    worship you give,
    and commitment you show,
    in word and deed.
The Lord grant you, this day and always,
    a clear vision,
    a living hope,
    and a constant faith,
    that you may live and work faithfully,
    to his glory.
Amen.

3
Blessing of a candidate for believer's baptism

May God who has called you to faith
    bless you now and always,
    filling you with love
    that you in turn might be a blessing to others.
May the joy you have found in him continue to burn,
    faith continue to grow,
    and light continue to shine,
    your life and witness testifying daily
    to his grace.

May his word guide you,
>   his power equip you,
>   his grace renew you,
>   and his love enfold you,
>   so that the commitment you express today
>   will endure undiminished tomorrow and every day,
>   through Jesus Christ our Lord.
Amen.

4
Blessing of youth workers/Sunday school staff

God guide, equip, and prosper you
>   in your sacred calling.
May he speak not just *through* you
>   but also *to* you
>   as you work and witness,
>   share and support,
>   instruct and enable.
May the energy of youth—
>   its enthusiasm,
>   openness,
>   idealism,
>   and sense of expectation—
>   invigorate your ministry,
>   sustain your faith,
>   and shape you and those in your charge,
>   through Jesus Christ our Lord.
Amen.

5
Blessing of a pastoral team

Through your listening may burdens be shared.
Through your speaking may comfort be given.
Through your actions may support be offered.
Through your care may hope be restored.
Through your love may faith be nurtured.
Through your touch may worth be affirmed.
Through all you do and all you are
   may Christ be present—
   his compassion expressed and goodness
   experienced—
   his kingdom brought closer,
   on earth as it is in heaven.
Amen.

6
Blessing of a healing team

The love of Christ flow within you,
   that you may be a channel of his Spirit
   and a conduit of his saving grace.
The compassion of Christ fill you,
   that you may express his care
   and bring his healing touch.
The might of Christ work through you,
   that you may impart his strength
   and release his renewing power.
The purpose of Christ be furthered by you,
   that, in our broken and bleeding world,
   you may minister his peace, joy, hope, and wholeness,
   to his glory.
Amen.

7
Blessing of church cleaners

God bless you in the special service you offer,
　　all too often unheralded,
　　unacknowledged,
　　unrecognized,
　　yet making so vital a contribution to our life together.
Seen or unseen,
　　appreciated or taken for granted,
　　may you find fulfillment in your ministry—
　　God encouraging, enthusing, and equipping you
　　through the knowledge that in serving others
　　you also serve him.
Amen.

8
Blessing of a catering team

Bless you for the sustenance you give,
　　the refreshment you provide,
　　the hospitality you afford,
　　and the fellowship you foster.
Bless you for the consecration of your gifts,
　　the offering of your time,
　　and the giving of your labor—
　　the buying, cooking, preparing, and serving
　　that makes possible so many events in which we share.
As you minister to us,
　　so may God minister to you,
　　blessing you in body, mind, and spirit,
　　through Jesus Christ our Lord.
Amen.

9
Blessing of a new vicar

May God speak *to* you and *through* you.
May Christ shine *in* you and *from* you.
May the Spirit be *upon* you and *with* you.
May wisdom guide your thoughts,
    truth mark your words,
    and love inspire your deeds,
    so that you may fulfil your calling
    and honor your trust.
The blessing of God,
    Father, Son, and Holy Spirit,
    be with you now
    and continue each day to fill and thrill you.
Amen.

10
Blessing of a new curate

Christ take your willingness to learn
    and readiness to serve.
Christ use your eagerness and enthusiasm,
    energy and ideas.
Christ shape your thoughts, words, and deeds,
    your attitude and aspirations,
    faith and character.
Christ draw near to *us* through *you*
    and to *you* through *us*,
    as together we strive to walk his way
    and advance his kingdom,
    to his glory.
Amen.

11
Blessing of a new ordinand/trainee minister

May God guide you in the days ahead,
    speaking his word
    and helping you to listen.
May he probe
    and enable you to consider,
    challenge
    and equip you to respond.
May he deepen your faith,
    enlarge your vision,
    and strengthen your commitment,
    granting you wisdom, humility,
    and openness in all you do,
    a hunger to learn,
    desire to grow,
    and resolve to serve.
God bless you and those whom you love,
    as you honor his call
    and seek his will for the future,
    through Jesus Christ our Lord.
Amen.

12
Blessing of a vicar leaving for a new parish
(*Name*),
>as you prepare for a new stage in your journey of life
>and path of discipleship,
>may God go with you.

May he honor the time you have spent here,
>that it may carry on bearing fruit
>in the months and years ahead—
>a lasting legacy of your work—
>and may the way you have helped to shape
>the journey and path of others
>be a source of inspiration both to them and you
>in times to come.

God use you in your continued ministry,
>to make known his mercy,
>impart his joy,
>share his peace,
>and express his love,
>in Christ's name.

Amen.

13
Blessing of lay readers/deacons/elders/church wardens

Faith be yours,
>wisdom, vision, and energy,
>that you may be equipped to lead.

Love be yours,
>compassion, gentleness, and humility,
>that you may be equipped to serve.

Insight be yours,
>patience, perseverance, and dedication,
>that you may be equipped to release the gifts of others.

God's grace be upon you,
 Christ's love work within you,
 and the Spirit's power flow through you,
 that you may faithfully share
 in nurturing and building the Church.
Amen.

14
Blessing of a church choir/choristers

God take your love of song and delight in melody,
 and weave your voices into a tapestry of worship
 and collage of praise.
May the gift of music you dedicate today
 enrich our sense of praise and wonder,
 gratitude and celebration,
 the harmony of hymns and anthems leading us
 to a deeper awareness of God
 and of his presence among us,
 so that, our hearts at one with him
 and our lives in tune with his will,
 we may sing together a new song,
 to his glory.
Amen.

15
Blessing of a church music group

Through your voices and instruments
    may God be honored.
Through your music and song
    may worship be offered.
Through the talents you consecrate today
    may hearts be uplifted,
    reaching up in heartfelt adoration
    and joyful praise.
God grant his blessing *upon* you
    and *through* you,
    to the glory of his name.
Amen.

The wider Church

16
Commissioning of a new missionary

Go …
    to give
    and receive,
    to teach
    and learn,
    to speak
    and listen,
    to serve
    and be served.
Go …
    not to *take* Christ with you,
    but to embody his presence
    and to meet him in others,
    sharing with him and them
    in the continuing journey of faith.
Amen.

17
Commissioning of an industrial chaplain

Reach out into the varied world of industry,
    recognizing it is God's world too.
Minister, by his grace,
    in the noise and bustle,
    the routine and repetition,
    the automation and technology,
    the tensions and camaraderie,
    the decline and change,
    the research and development—
    showing that in this world of work
    God is at work as well.
Amen.

18
Commissioning of a hospital chaplain

May Christ the healer reach out
    through your service and ministry,
    bringing courage where there is fear,
    hope where there is despair,
    comfort where there is sorrow,
    strength where there is suffering,
    peace where there is turmoil,
    and faith where there is doubt.
May his grace go with you,
    his light shine in you,
    his love flow from you,
    and his power work through you.
Amen.

19
Commissioning of a hospice chaplain

Christ of Gethsemane be with you
 as you reach out to those crushed by fear and sorrow.
Christ of the cross move in you
 as you minister to those enduring pain
 in body, mind, and spirit.
Christ of the tomb inspire you
 as you support the dying
 and bring comfort to those who mourn.
Christ of the resurrection work through you,
 to bring light in darkness,
 hope in despair,
 peace in confusion,
 and life out of death.
Christ bless you and all you serve,
 now and always.
Amen.

20
Commissioning of an armed forces chaplain

In peace or conflict,
 routine maneuver or active service,
 may you reflect Christ's love,
 and make him known through your life and ministry.
May his Spirit equip you to inspire and uplift,
 comfort and reassure,
 nourish and nurture,
 challenge and enrich,
 so that, in the harsh realities and tensions of this world,
 you may offer a glimpse of something deeper—
 a sense of purpose worth living for,
 and, if necessary, worth *dying* for.
Amen.

21
Commissioning of a university/college chaplain

May God equip you, by his grace,
   to reach out in love,
   offering to those seeking knowledge,
   insight and understanding
   a glimpse of Christ,
   the way, the truth, and the life.
May God grant you a wise tongue,
   a listening ear,
   a loving heart,
   and a sensitive spirit,
   so that you may help lead those to whom you minister
   into a deeper awareness of your love for them
   and for all,
   through Jesus Christ our Lord.
Amen.

The wider world

22
Blessing of a newly conceived child

For the miracle of life and the wonder of creation,
    Lord, we praise you.
For the love that has led to the conception of this child,
    and the sense of joy and anticipation it has brought,
    Lord, we thank you.
For the days and months ahead—
    of growth and development in the womb,
    of labor and delivery,
    nurturing and nourishing,
    infancy, childhood, and beyond—
    Lord, we worship you.
Grant your guidance,
    your strength,
    your joy,
    your blessing,
    through Jesus Christ our Lord.
Amen.

23
Blessing of a miscarried child

Receive, Lord, this child,
    taken from us so suddenly and painfully,
    before love could fully be expressed,
    relationships built,
    or dreams fulfilled,
    yet nonetheless meaning so much in so many ways.
Support *[parents' names*]* through this time,
    in all the sorrow, pain, and confusion they feel,
    and help them somehow to deal with their loss
    and find strength and hope to face the future.

*Or parent's name in case of a single mother

Take their little one (*use name if given*),
    and grant *him/her* joy, peace, and blessing
    in your eternal kingdom,
    through Jesus Christ our Lord.
Amen.

24
Blessing of a stillborn child

In the heartbreak of broken dreams
    and shattered expectations,
    the numbness of shock and disbelief,
    the ache of grief and despair,
    the pain of loss and bereavement,
    may your love, Lord, somehow bring strength,
    support,
    courage,
    and comfort.
Receive this little one into your eternal care,
    and assure us of your purpose beyond death itself,
    through Jesus Christ our Lord.
Amen.

25
Blessing of a newborn child

God be praised for the joy you have brought
    and the delight that surrounds you.
God provide for and protect you,
    granting you health,
    wisdom,
    peace,
    and joy.
God guide your footsteps,
    and equip you for your journey, wherever it might lead.
God be with those who love you,
    and those you will love in turn,
    that you and they will taste his goodness
    and celebrate the life he offers in all its fullness,
    through Jesus Christ our Lord.
Amen.

26
Blessing of a premature child

Lord Jesus Christ,
    born as a baby into a hostile and dangerous world,
    watch over this little one,
    so vulnerable yet so precious,
    so tiny yet carrying such hopes
    and inspiring such enormous love.
Cherish, protect, support, and strengthen,
    so that *[Name]* may grow in health and strength,
    wisdom and maturity,
    experiencing joy
    and bringing it to others.
In your name we pray.
Amen.

27
Blessing of a mentally disabled child

[Name],
    may God watch over you,
    granting you the care, support,
    love, and provision you need.
May he give wisdom, dedication,
    help, and strength to your parents
    and to all who will look after you,
    and through the loving, patient nurture
    that surrounds you,
    may you find inner pleasure,
    peace,
    security,
    and true contentment.
Amen.

28
Blessing of a physically disabled child

Almighty God,
    though disability will bring difficulty,
    give *[Name]* strength to overcome it,
    helping *her/him* to find joy, blessing, and fulfillment
    in all life holds.
Grant *her/him* patience,
    courage,
    resilience,
    and determination,
    and, above all, the knowledge that *s/he*
    is a unique person,
    precious in *her/his* own right,
    a whole person with as much to contribute
    as anyone.
In that assurance may *s/he* live each moment.
Amen.

29
Blessing of a child with learning difficulties

Loving God,
    watch over *[Name]*
    and grant *her/him* the care,
    encouragement,
    and provision *s/he* needs to realize *her/his* potential.
Through the devotion of parent/s and family,
    the support of friends,
    and the dedication of teachers,
    instill self-belief,
    enthusiasm,
    resilience,
    and resourcefulness,
    equipping *her/him* to meet the challenges ahead,
    through Jesus Christ our Lord.
Amen.

30
Blessing of a child starting school

May God bless you, *[Name]*,
    in the time you will spend at school,
    and equip you through it
    with the resources you need for the journey of life.
May you find pleasure in learning,
    enrichment through friendships,
    and fun through shared activities,
    your education helping you to grow
    not only in knowledge but also as a person.
God protect you from harm,
    equip you with wisdom,
    and enfold you in love,
    granting you joy now
    and fulfillment in the years to come,
    through Jesus Christ our Lord.
Amen.

31
Blessing of a young person before an examination

At this stressful time, Lord,
   grant your peace—
   composure of mind
   and serenity of spirit—
   that the long hours of work, study, and revision
   leading up to this exam
   may bear fruit,
   receiving their due reward.
Help *[Name]* simply to give of *his/her* best,
   and, having done that, to rest content,
   knowing that no one could ask for more.
In your name we ask it.
Amen.

32
Blessing of a son or daughter leaving home

God bless you, *[Name]*, for the joy you've brought,
   the help you've given
   and love you've shared—
   everything you've contributed to this home and family
   in so many ways
   across so many years.
As you travel now from the old to the new,
   wherever you might be and whatever life might bring,
   may God go with you—
   a light to your path
   and a companion along your way—
   his hand there to guide and his arms to embrace,
   bringing the knowledge
   that you are as close to his heart
   as you will always be to ours.
Amen.

33
Blessing of parents/a parent
when a daughter or son leaves home

May God be with you at this time of change,
 in the contrasting emotions you feel—
 the pride . . .
 and the pain,
 the love . . .
 and the loss,
 the sense of responsibility fulfilled . . .
 but also of a chapter closing.
May he help you to let go . . .
 yet also stay close,
 to keep in contact . . .
 yet also leave space;
 to be there when needed . . .
 yet also to let *[Name]* make *her/his* own decisions,
 finding joy in *her/his* freedom . . .
 but equally in your own,
 discovering new avenues for your love,
 new uses for your time,
 and new directions in your life,
 God walking with you and all you hold dear,
 this and every day.
Amen.

34
Blessing of a first-year university/college student

Grant to *[Name]*, Lord, at this exciting yet daunting time,
 this time of embracing the new
 and moving on from the old,
 a sure and certain knowledge of your presence,
 your guidance,
 and your love that, come what may, will not fail.
Grant the ability to work but also to rest,
 to study but also to socialize,

to embrace new insights but also to keep hold of truth,
to welcome all that is good in student life
but also to resist whatever is bad,
knowing when to say yes, and when to say no.
Watch over *[Name]*,
equip and enable *him/her*
for all the challenges and opportunities that lie ahead,
and so may *he/she* find true fulfillment,
now and in the years ahead.
Amen.

35
Blessing of someone starting a new job

Be present, Lord, at this time of mixed emotions—
anxiety yet anticipation,
uncertainty yet eagerness—
and grant the assurance that
whatever this new job might bring,
and whatever the future may hold,
you will be there in it,
guiding,
equipping,
supplying,
and sustaining.
Through work done,
friendships made,
challenges faced,
and goals realized
may *[Name]* find fulfillment
and receive your blessing,
in Christ's name.
Amen.

36
Blessing of someone on *her/his* retirement
Father God,
  grant that this time of endings
  may also be one of new beginnings,
  of exploring new horizons and discovering fresh joys.
May it bring opportunities
  for well-earned rest and relaxation,
  but equally for using gifts and skills in different ways—
  the chance to do things long dreamt of, which,
  up to now,
  time or circumstances have made impossible.
May memories of the past bring pleasure
  and hopes for the future bring anticipation,
  years of experience being complemented
  by a youthful spirit,
  a mind that is ever young at heart.
In all that is yet to come,
  bring happiness, peace,
  love, and fulfillment,
  through Jesus Christ our Lord.
Amen.

37
Blessing of a new home

Be present in this home, Lord,
   and fill it with laughter, love, peace, and pleasure.
May it be a place of harmony, happiness,
   warmth, and welcome,
   bringing enduring contentment and lasting memories.
Watch over all who live here,
   protecting, nurturing, guiding, and providing,
   so that it may be not just a house
   but, above all, a home—
   a place of joy touched by your presence
   and sanctified by your grace,
   through Jesus Christ our Lord.
Amen.

38
Blessing of a person or family moving away

At this time of excitement yet apprehension,
   hopes for the future mingled with memories of the past,
   grant, Lord, the knowledge that wherever we may go,
   and whatever life may bring,
   you are with us,
   looking always to guide, strengthen, and bless.
May everything that *[Name(s)] has/have* shared
   and enjoyed here
   be remembered with thanksgiving and affection,
   but may it also prove a stepping stone into a new chapter,
   bringing celebration, laughter,
   peace, and fulfillment—
   each day illumined by the light of your grace
   and the radiance of your love.
Amen.

39
Blessing of an engagement ring

Gracious God,
    bless this ring and all it symbolizes—
    the love it represents,
    joy it articulates,
    commitment it proclaims,
    hopes, plans, and dreams it embodies.
May that love continue to flourish,
    that joy be deepened and enriched,
    that commitment hold firm
    in the changing fortunes of life
    and those dreams be realized,
    through Jesus Christ our Lord.
Amen.

40
Blessing of a couple on the start of completion of premarital counseling

God of all,
    devoted to us and delighting in our happiness,
    grant your blessing on *this couple/these couples.**
May their relationship grow stronger each day,
    their love deeper
    and commitment surer.
Put your love in their hearts,
    so that, whatever the future may hold,
    they may continue to find joy and fulfillment
    in each other,
    holding fast together through laughter or tears,
    sunshine or storm,
    through Jesus Christ our Lord.
Amen.

*Use names if preferred

41
A wedding blessing—for bride and groom (1)

May God's love enfold and engulf you
    so that it may flow through your veins,
    uniting and shaping you in all you are and do.
May your love for each other be as real as his for you—
    as deep as the deepest sea,
    as bright as the brightest star,
    as strong as the strongest bond,
    and as pure as the purest gold—
    so that what you celebrate today will endure tomorrow
    and for all eternity,
    through Jesus Christ our Lord.
Amen.

42
A wedding blessing—for bride and groom (2)

In your living and loving,
    thinking and doing,
    working and sharing,
    may God be with you.
In your laughing and weeping together—
    your joys and sorrows,
    dreams and disappointments,
    pleasure and pain—
    may you find fulfillment.
In all the present offers
    and everything the future brings
    may God richly bless you.
Amen.

43
Blessing of a new parent

May the delight you feel today
    continue to fill and thrill you in the years ahead,
    the privilege of nurturing a young life—
    supporting and guiding,
    protecting and providing—
    offering a constant source of joy.
In the demands and duties of daily life,
    may there always be time to listen,
    share,
    encourage,
    and enjoy—
    time to appreciate the unique and priceless treasure of parenthood.
God's blessing be upon you and your little one,
    this and every day,
    through Jesus Christ our Lord.
Amen.

44
Blessing on the renewal of wedding vows

God go with you on your continuing journey together.
May all you have shared
    equip you for all that is yet to come—
    past mistakes learned from,
    past achievements built on,
    past disagreements put behind you,
    past promises re-expressed.
May love continue to grow,
    trust to flourish,
    fulfillment to increase,
    and joy to blossom,
    through Jesus Christ our Lord.
Amen.

45
Blessing of replacement wedding rings

Gracious God,
    we praise you for the love between this couple—
    still strong,
    still vibrant,
    still growing.
We thank you that though rings may need replacing,
    the union they symbolize is as real as ever,
    and so we consecrate these to you now,
    asking that they may be a visible sign
    of the continuing love, joy, fulfillment, and delight
    [Name] and *[Name]* have found in each other.
In Christ's name we pray.
Amen.

46
**Blessing at a silver, ruby, golden,
or diamond wedding celebration**

For the love we celebrate today—
    the mutual commitment across the years,
    the working, sharing, and building together
    through good times and bad,
    hopes and fears,
    joys and sorrows—
    we give glad and heartfelt thanks.
May that love,
    that bond,
    that closeness
    bless and enrich you as surely in the days to come
    as in the years gone by,
    and may God go with you,
    now and always.
Amen.

47
Blessing of the elderly

Eternal God,
   reach out in love,
   and support those for whom advancing years
   bring trials.
Though health may fade and faculties fail,
   strength decline and vigor wane,
   grant the assurance that your grace is the same
   yesterday, today, and tomorrow,
   a fixed point in a world of change.
So, then, in your mercy,
   grant help and strength,
   comfort and joy,
   and, above all, confidence in your enduring purpose—
   the knowledge that,
   come what may,
   your love will never let us go.
Amen.

48
Blessing of the sick

The compassion of Christ enfold you.
The arms of Christ support you.
The peace of Christ engulf you.
The grace of Christ sustain you.
The Spirit of Christ renew you.
The power of Christ make you whole.
Amen.

49
Blessing before an operation

The Lord soothe your spirit and calm your fears.
The Lord touch your body and grant strength.
The Lord bless this operation and bring healing.
Come, Lord,

and through your Spirit rest upon *[patient's name]*,
   upon the surgeon and team operating upon *her/him*,
   upon the nursing and support staff,
   upon this hospital in its healing ministry.
Work through all to fulfil your purpose
   and display your love,
   for your name's sake.
Amen.

50
Blessing of an AIDS sufferer

Caring and compassionate God,
   support *[Name]* in the trauma and turmoil of AIDS.
When terror suffocates,
   grant your peace.
When despair overwhelms,
   renew hope.
When vigor wanes,
   bring healing.
When rejection isolates,
   draw close.
Give help to wrestle with this disease,
   and still feel whole;
   to meet with fear and suspicion,
   yet still love;
   to confront the specter of death,
   yet still celebrate life.
Support,
   equip,
   and bless,
   this day and always,
   in Christ's name.
Amen.

51
Blessing of an Alzheimer's sufferer

In moments of confusion,
    God keep you safe.
In moments of clarity,
    God grant you joy.
In moments of frustration,
    God give you peace.
In moments of sorrow,
    God bring you comfort.
May he who sees into the secret places of your mind,
    beyond the devastation of this disease
    to the person that is you,
    encircle you in his arms,
    until that day when all is made new
    in his eternal kingdom,
    through Jesus Christ our Lord.
Amen.

52
Blessing of the terminally ill

God equip you to face the prospect of death,
    yet still celebrate life;
    to wrestle with despair,
    yet still hold on to hope;
    to cope with sorrow,
    yet still find joy;
    to bear pain,
    yet still embrace pleasure;
    to experience fear,
    yet still know peace;
    to be broken,

   yet still be whole;
   to face endings,
   yet still look forward to new beginnings,
   trusting that nothing can finally separate you
   from his love
   through Jesus Christ our Lord.
Amen.

53
Blessing of the dying

May Christ who, in anguish,
   wrestled with the prospect of suffering and death,
   support you in facing sorrow.
May Christ who endured thorns and nails
   piercing his flesh,
   and the agony of crucifixion,
   strengthen you in bearing pain.
May Christ who surrendered his spirit
   and breathed his last,
   accompany you in the shadow of death.
May Christ who rose again,
   triumphant over the grave,
   lead you into his eternal kingdom.
May Christ bless and keep you as you journey *with* him,
   and *to* him.
Amen.

54
Blessing for the victim of a sudden or violent death

After shock and trauma,
    bring, Lord, your peace and blessing:
    peace such as this world cannot give,
    blessing beyond anything we can ever ask or imagine,
    each enduring for all eternity—
    nothing ever again,
    in heaven or on earth,
    able to hurt, destroy, or overshadow your great love,
    through Jesus Christ our Lord.
Amen.

55
A funeral blessing—for the deceased

Go on your way, *[Name],* to new horizons,
    new life,
    new beginnings.
Go with our thanks for all you have meant to us
    and will continue to mean;
    for all you have contributed to our lives
    in ways great and small.
Go to the one who created you,
    who welcomes you now
    and whose arms will enfold you always.
Go in peace until we meet again
    and share once more,
    never again to be parted.
Amen.

56
A funeral service—at close of service

In your tears may God give comfort;
   in your turmoil, peace;
   in your darkness, light;
   in your despair, hope;
   in your weakness, strength;
   in your fear, confidence;
   in your loneliness, support;
   in your pain, relief;
   and at *your* death, life;
   through Jesus Christ our Lord.
Amen.

57
A graveside blessing

A chapter is closed, Lord;
   another just opened.
Life is over;
   it is only just starting.
The day is ended;
   but it has only just begun.
With grief, then, yet with gratitude,
   with heavy hearts, yet filled with hope,
   we entrust *[Name]* and ourselves
   into your sure keeping,
   confident that though all else may fail,
   you will not.
Amen.

58
A cremation blessing

Gracious God,
> bringer of life out of the dust,
> new life out of the ashes,
> we commit *[Name]* and ourselves
> into your loving and everlasting arms.

In life or in death,
> bless us by your renewing power and restoring touch,
> and lead us into your eternal kingdom,
> through Jesus Christ our Lord.

Amen.

59
Blessing during the interment of ashes

God's blessing be upon you, *[Name]*,
> for everything you have meant and will always mean.

Bless you for happiness shared:
> laughter, pleasure, jubilation;
> for occasions shared:
> holidays, anniversaries, celebrations;
> for difficulties shared:
> disappointments, problems, crises;
> for closeness shared:
> love, friendship, commitment.

For all we have gone through together,
> and all we will share in life to come,
> God's blessing be upon you.

Amen.

60
Blessing during the scattering of ashes

Lord of life,
   for all this place meant to *[Name]*, we thank you,
   for all *[Name]* meant to us, we praise you,
   for all *s/he* will always mean in our hearts,
   we acknowledge you,
   for all *s/he* means still to you, we worship you.
We return *[Name]* to you,
   remembering that though we scatter now these ashes in fond farewell,
   your love lives on and purpose continues.
Bless *[Name]*,
   bless us,
   through Jesus Christ our Lord.
Amen.

Society

61
Blessing for the police

May God guide and prosper you in your work,
   helping you to enforce justice
   and to promote stability and security
   within the community you serve.
May he protect you from danger,
   provide you with courage,
   imbue you with integrity,
   and endow you with strength,
   so that you may discharge your responsibilities wisely and fairly,
   honoring the trust shown in you,
   to the good of all,
   through Jesus Christ our Lord.
Amen.

62
Blessing for firefighters

Sovereign God,
>watch over not only those here today
>but equally firefighters everywhere
>in the difficult and often dangerous work
>they undertake.

Grant them skill in all they do,
>courage when it means putting their safety at risk,
>protection from accident and injury,
>stamina in the harrowing
>and demanding situations they so often face.

Strengthen them in times of crisis,
>guide them in moments of uncertainty,
>and minister to them in experiences of trauma.

Equip them with the resources they need,
>so that, confidently, safely, and effectively,
>they may continue the vital service they offer,
>through Jesus Christ our Lord.

Amen.

63
Blessing for ambulance staff and paramedics

God of love and compassion,
>grant your blessing
>on all involved in ambulance service—
>paramedics,
>support staff,
>drivers,
>mechanics, and technicians—
>all those whose dedication and skills are vital
>in providing a service we so much take for granted.

Enthuse,
   equip,
   and enable them in all they do,
   providing them with the resources they need—
   physical, emotional, and spiritual—
   to continue their ministry
   of healing, supporting, and comforting.
Work through them to express your loving care,
   through Jesus Christ our Lord.
Amen.

64
Blessing for a GP

In your work of examining and diagnosis,
   may God grant you wisdom.
In your task of prescribing and treating,
   may he grant you skill.
In your ministry of listening and counseling,
   may he grant you insight.
In everything you do,
   may God work through you,
   to heal and help,
   relieve and reassure,
   safeguard and support,
   his presence bringing you motivation,
   joy,
   and fulfillment in your calling,
   through Jesus Christ our Lord.
Amen.

65
Blessing for a nurse

Living God,
    we commit *[Name]* to you,
    asking your blessing upon *her/his* work.
Through care given,
    treatment administered,
    reassurance offered,
    and understanding shown,
    reach out to those in *her/his* care,
    bringing healing and wholeness,
    renewal in body, mind, and spirit.
Give skill, diligence, patience, and compassion
    in all *s/he* does
    through *her/his* ministry giving expression
    to your love for all,
    through Jesus Christ our Lord.
Amen.

66
Blessing for a caregiver

[Name],
    in your devoted but demanding ministry,
    may you receive God's blessing
    and be a blessing in turn to the one you care for.
When exhaustion overwhelms you,
    may God renew your vigor.
When patience is tested,
    may he grant fortitude.
When all seems bleak,
    may he shed light.
When tears flow,
    may he bring comfort.

May you and your loved one know his peace,
>   receive his strength,
>   and experience his love,
>   surrounding and supporting you always,
>   through Jesus Christ our Lord.
Amen.

67
Blessing for members of the armed forces

Sovereign God,
>   bless this *platoon/battalion/brigade/regiment/etc.*
>   and all who serve within it.
Equip each member with the skills, fitness,
>   reserves, and resources they need
>   to fulfill the missions set for them,
>   not seeking war or glorifying violence,
>   but fighting evil where necessary,
>   confronting oppression,
>   combating terror,
>   and working for a just and lasting peace.
Protect from danger,
>   and give help in adversity,
>   courage in moments of fear,
>   and coolness in times of crisis,
>   enfolding these and their loved ones
>   in your gracious care, this day and always.
Amen.

68
Blessing for fishermen

God's eye watch over your boat,
   his power control the sea,
   his hand enrich your work,
   and his arms embrace your loved ones.
In rain or sunshine,
   calm or storm,
   may he be with you and those you cherish,
   guiding,
   prospering,
   protecting,
   through Jesus Christ our Lord.
Amen.

69
Blessing for a farm/farmers

Loving God,
   grant your blessing on this farm—
   this land, home, and livelihood—
   and on all whose future is interwoven with its fortunes.
Give *vigor/contentment* to the *crops/animals*,
   conditions that promote strong and healthy growth.
Give skill and sensitivity in husbandry,
   the quest for productivity balanced
   by respect for your creation.
Give guidance in managing natural resources,
   the ability to steward them wisely for the good of all.
Provide, protect,
   equip, and encourage,
   bringing joy in times of fruitfulness
   and support when days are hard,
   through Jesus Christ our Lord.
Amen.

70
Blessing for teachers

God grant you wisdom to teach,
   sensitivity to encourage,
   skill to enthuse,
   strength to discipline,
   and patience to persevere.
May he keep your vision fresh,
   your mind hungry,
   and your motivation strong,
   enabling you to capture the imagination
   of those you teach,
   getting the best from them
   and helping each to realize their full potential.
May he grant you joy and fulfillment in your work,
   that through it you may be a blessing to others in turn,
   for Christ's sake.
Amen.

71
Blessing for shop workers

God bless you in the work you do,
   that in the service you offer,
   the camaraderie you share,
   the people you meet,
   and the money you earn
   you may find interest, enjoyment, and satisfaction
   today and in the days ahead.
Amen.

72
Blessing for factory workers

Living God,
>recognizing you are as much Lord of daily life
as of Sunday worship,
as much involved in the mundane as the "sacred,"
so we commit this place to you
and all who will be employed here—
those on production lines and the shop floor,
supervisors and managers,
accounts, sales, and marketing teams,
drivers, engineers, and technicians,
office and support staff—
their contribution vital to the viability of this factory,
the product it manufactures,
and the jobs it makes possible.
Seen or unseen,
acknowledged or unacknowledged,
work here, through your Spirit,
in labor relations,
in banter and camaraderie,
in health and safety,
and in work honestly done and honestly rewarded.
In Christ's name we pray.

Amen.

73
Blessing for office workers

Living Lord,
   put your hand upon all who work in this building.
In the busy world of commerce,
   amid the telephone calls, faxes, emails, and letters,
   the piles of paperwork,
   the endless tasks of filing, assessing,
   analysing, and decision making,
   give a daily reminder of the people behind it all—
   the human face of colleagues
   and of those behind the records, forms,
   orders, and correspondence.
Guide all dealings here,
   and grant that,
   however intense the pressures of work,
   tedium of routine,
   demand for profit,
   or pull of personal ambition,
   there will always be time for others,
   a recognition that each is not just a name or number
   but an individual,
   a person in their own right,
   valued by you
   and so to be valued by all.
Amen.

74
Blessing for a school assembly
Be present in this school, Lord,
    granting your blessing on teachers,
    support staff,
    children, and parents alike.
Promote here eagerness to learn,
    desire to give of one's best,
    respect for all,
    a sense of community and togetherness.
Instruct,
    enable,
    enthuse,
    encourage,
    and enfold all in your constant love,
    through Jesus Christ our Lord.
Amen.

Buildings

Church-related

75
Consecration of a church sanctuary

Sovereign God,
> we consecrate these bricks and mortar,
> fittings and furnishings,
> to you,
> as a sacred space,
> hallowed ground set aside for praise and worship,
> preaching and teaching,
> word and sacrament.

Move in this place,
> drawing near to us as we draw near to you,
> so that, by your grace,
> we may grow each day as your church,
> this building a visible sign of our life together,
> a symbol of the service and witness we offer
> in your name.

Amen.

76
Consecration of a church hall

Lord of life,
  bless this hall and all it will be used for.
May it be a place of coming together,
  sharing,
  and befriending;
  a place of refreshment and relaxation;
  a place of service both to us and others,
  used as a resource in our fellowship
  and wider community.
May we meet you as much here as in worship,
  through the fellowship we enjoy,
  the events we arrange,
  and the activities we hold,
  your presence being seen among us in all we are
  and all we do,
  through Jesus Christ our Lord.
Amen.

77
Consecration of Sunday school facilities

Sovereign God,
  together with this new *room/building/resource*,
  we consecrate to you today
  the young people of this church,
  asking that you will make known your love to them,
  speaking powerfully to youthful hearts and minds
  of your presence, power, and purpose—
  your awesome grace that yearns to bless and enrich,
  and to lead young and old alike
  into the joy of life eternal.
Equip those in this church entrusted with the task
  of communicating the gospel,
  all who in any way contribute to youth work among us.

Reach out through their words and deeds
to nourish and nurture,
provide and prepare,
your joy and peace touching the lives
of those in their charge,
through Jesus Christ our Lord.
Amen.

78
Consecration of day care facilities

Lord Jesus Christ,
remembering again how you welcomed children
to your side,
so we commit now this day care facility to you
as a symbol of the welcome and commitment
that we would extend in turn
to babies, toddlers, and parents here,
showing them that they are valued among us,
their needs recognized and met as fully as possible.
Consecrate this room, we pray—
the resources it holds,
all who will staff it
and the children who will spend time here—
that the simple but vital ministry offered here
may contribute in a special way
to the life of this church.
May your care, joy, and blessing pervade all,
to your glory.
Amen.

79
Consecration of a church extension

Living God,
   with gratitude for all that has made it possible
   we commit this extension to you,
   asking that through it you will help us—
   wisely, generously, creatively, and lovingly—
   to speak of Christ and serve him more effectively.
May these enlarged premises inspire us in turn
   to enlarge our vision,
   seeking a deeper understanding of your greatness,
   a fuller grasp of your love,
   a richer appreciation of your goodness,
   and a heightened sense of all you seek to do,
   in and through us,
   in the life of this church and neighborhood.
May bricks and mortar speak to us of hearts and minds,
   consecrated to and won for you,
   through Jesus Christ our Lord.
Amen.

80
Consecration of a church vestibule

Gracious God,
   we consecrate this vestibule to you,
   asking that,
   as well as being an entrance,
   it will be a sanctified space,
   the welcome people are offered here
   speaking of love, care, and acceptance;
   the signs, posters, notices, and literature displayed
   pointing to a vibrant inner life
   matched by an equal resolve to reach out

to you and to others
in living worship and committed service.
May all who pass through these doors
immediately recognize you are here,
being drawn more deeply into your presence,
and returning to their daily lives,
knowing that you walk with them,
here and everywhere.
Amen.

81
Consecration of a church kitchen

Loving God,
we commit this kitchen to you,
conscious that so much of importance
to our life together begins here—
the preparing of refreshments after worship,
social events,
shared meals, and a host of other occasions;
the tasks of clearing and washing up afterward,
the preparing of flowers,
the weekly routine of cleaning.
Bless this room,
and those who offer such faithful service here—
all too often and easily overlooked,
yet so vital to the fellowship we share—
that they in turn may be a blessing to us and to others,
in Christ's name.
Amen.

82
Consecration of a church office

Lord God,
>we bring you the administration of this church,
>recognizing its importance to healthy fellowship,
>effective outreach,
>and ongoing worship—
>so much that we do and offer
>calling for unsung but indispensable work
>behind the scenes:
>the consecrated use of skills, time, and resources
>in your service.

Hallow, then, this office by your grace,
>that all the work undertaken within it
>may be offered not simply as duty or routine
>but as an act of service,
>furthering our life and witness here,
>ministering to our practical needs,
>and, above all, contributing to the fulfillment
>of your loving purpose,
>through Jesus Christ our Lord.

Amen.

83
Consecration of a local ecumenical project

Sovereign God,
>may the vision that has called this project into being
>burn brightly in the years ahead,
>whatever theological, political,
>or practical challenges may confront it.

When the daily reality of living and working together
>throws up complications,
>when unforeseen issues expose differences
>and disagreements,
>may the knowledge of what unites us—

the all-embracing love of Christ—
prove more compelling than what divides,
offering ways to resolve conflict
and emerge stronger.
Shine through this place and your people here,
that they may be a living expression
of your reconciling purpose
and the harmony with you and one another
that you desire for us all.
Amen.

84
Consecration of an interfaith center

Holy God,
in a broken world,
torn by fear and hatred,
scarred by prejudice and intolerance,
may this place be a sign of hope,
a visible testimony to the healing power of your love.
Recognizing the differences in faith, creed, and culture
that divide us,
may we yet focus on what unites rather than divides,
the life and work of this center showing it is possible
to stay true to our traditions
but be open to each other,
to move beyond tolerance to respect,
beyond discord to dialogue,
beyond passive acceptance
to an active working together,
building bridges within a fragmented society,
healing the wounds,
and working for the good of all.
Amen.

In the wider world

85
Consecration of a school/classroom

Sovereign God,
  encircle this school with your love,
  touch it with your presence,
  surround it with your protection,
  and endow all within it with your wisdom.
Equip those who will teach here with the skills they need,
  with dedication to develop them
  and sensitivity in applying them,
  and may those in their charge find inspiration,
  encouragement, insight, and guidance.
Grant that, as well as being a place of learning,
  this may be an environment where friendships grow,
  confidence is built,
  characters are fashioned,
  and skills are learned for daily life,
  through Jesus Christ our Lord.
Amen.

86
Consecration of a hospital/hospital ward

Compassionate God,
  sanctify this hospital with your renewing touch.
Equip, encourage, and enable those who will work here—
  from consultants, clinicians, nurses, and chaplains
  to cleaners, caterers, porters, and support staff—
  that all may contribute in bringing healing and wholeness
  in body, mind, and spirit.
Minister to those who will come here as patients,
  and, in your love, reach out
  into the contrasting circumstances they will face—
  the joy of childbirth and heartbreak of bereavement,

the delight of recovery and shock of bleak diagnoses,
    the exhilaration of an all-clear and trauma of surgery—
    so much hope and despair,
    faith and fear,
    so many joys and sorrows,
    beginnings and endings.
Be present in it all, Lord,
    to hold and help,
    strengthen and support,
    granting in sickness or in health, life or death,
    the knowledge that you will be there, come what may.
Amen.

87
Consecration of a nursing/residential care home

Eternal God,
    reach into this home
    and fill it with the light of your presence
    and the glow of your love.
Though residents here are in their twilight years,
    many wrestling with physical or mental decline,
    may there nonetheless be a celebration of life in this place,
    an appreciation of all that continues
    to be good and special,
    an atmosphere of community
    and a respect for the dignity and worth of all.
Work through the staff members here,
    whatever their role may be,
    filling them with gentleness, compassion,
    sensitivity, and understanding,
    that in giving they may receive,
    and in serving others they may serve you.
Amen.

88
Consecration of a psychiatric hospital/ward

Be present in this place, Lord,
    and, through the ministry it offers,
    grant peace to those in turmoil.
Protect and equip all who work here,
    in their demanding and sometimes dangerous work,
    and give them skill, patience, wisdom, and compassion,
    as they strive to bring relief
    to those in pain
    whose lives have been undermined or destroyed
    by drug abuse,
    personality disorder,
    depression, or psychological trauma.
Though so much seems to deny love and question faith,
    grant yet your help to calm the storm
    in suffering lives and minds,
    through Jesus Christ our Lord.
Amen.

89
Consecration of a hospice

Eternal God,
    amid the death, trauma, and sorrow
    that will inevitably touch this place,
    may there also be a celebration of what each day brings,
    an imparting of joy, love, and peace,
    and the bringing of hope,
    both now and in life to come.
Equip all who exercise their special ministry here
    with the emotional, physical,
    and spiritual reserves they need,
    and through them bring relief from pain,
    reassurance to the fearful,
    respite to caregivers,
    and comfort to all who grieve.

Grant through the therapy administered,
> the compassion shown,
> and the support offered,
> that all who spend their last days here
> may find quality in life
> and dignity in death,
> through Jesus Christ our Lord.
Amen.

90
Consecration of a homeless shelter

As one, Lord, who so often had nowhere to lay your head,
> reach out through this shelter
> to all in a similar plight today—
> youngsters who have run away from home,
> victims of abuse,
> those who abuse themselves,
> the poor and destitute,
> people of the street,
> alcoholics and drug addicts,
> those who have dropped out of society.

May they find here food and shelter,
> warmth and compassion,
> company and acceptance—
> the knowledge that they are not completely on their own,
> that someone, somewhere, cares.

Guide,
> protect,
> and enable all who serve here,
> and provide them with the resources they need
> to continue their work,
> and bring hope to those who society so easily forgets.
Amen.

91
Consecration of a prison

Lord Jesus Christ,
   work in this place
   and grant your blessing to all within it.
Give wisdom to the warden and staff—
   the ability to be firm but fair,
   strict but supportive,
   hard when necessary but human where possible—
   and to the inmates give true remorse
   and the desire to make amends—
   a resolve to use this time to move on from past mistakes
   and begin again.
In imprisonment, may they find true liberty,
   the freedom that you alone can bring,
   through your redeeming, renewing grace.
Amen.

92
Consecration of a new small business

Sovereign God,
   be with *[Name(s)]* in this new venture,
   granting help and guidance
   along the road that lies ahead.
Give wisdom to make right decisions,
   ability to cultivate necessary skills,
   and health to cope with the workload;
   give encouragement when business is slow
   and equanimity in times of disappointment,
   the vision needed to grasp opportunities,
   but also integrity when it is tempting to cut corners;
   above all, give discipline to do whatever must be done
   yet the ability also to switch off,
   recognizing that there must be time
   for rest and recreation,
   friends and loved ones.

Receive this business,
    and the livelihood it represents,
    into your hands,
    and grant your blessing,
    through Jesus Christ our Lord.
Amen.

93
Consecration of a supermarket

God of all,
    we consecrate this place to you,
    asking that in the bustle of everyday life,
    the routine of shopping,
    you will speak of your love
    but also of the needs and circumstances of others.
Through shelves piled high with food,
    remind us of how fortunate we are,
    how much we have to celebrate and thank you for.
Through the bewildering variety of produce,
    daily replenished,
    remind us of those, both near and far,
    whose livelihoods are interwoven with what is sold here,
    all too many so much less fortunate than ourselves;
    to them what we take for granted
    seeming unimaginable luxury, an impossible dream.
Recognized or unrecognized,
    speak to those who work and shop here
    of realities beyond themselves,
    highlighting blessings,
    quickening consciences,
    and inviting a response,
    through Jesus Christ our Lord.
Amen.

94
Consecration of a factory

Sovereign God,
   we commit this factory to you,
   asking that you will prosper it
   and be present in the decisions made,
   work undertaken,
   friendships formed,
   and lives of those employed here.
May it provide lasting jobs,
   security for families now and in years to come.
May it be wisely managed,
   upholding standards of health and safety,
   quality and service,
   fair trade,
   environmental responsibility,
   and employee relations.
And may its products contribute to others,
   promoting economic growth
   and, directly or indirectly,
   bringing pleasure to consumers.
All this we ask in Christ's name.
Amen.

95
Consecration of an office

In the work done here—
   decisions taken,
   plans made,
   business implemented;
   in the people employed here—
   management,
   personnel,
   auxiliaries;
   in the lives influenced here—
   customers,
   clients,
   or claimants;
   be present, Lord,
   to guide, bless, and prosper,
   through Jesus Christ our Lord.
Amen.

Church Fittings and Furnishings

If the item to be consecrated has been bought in memory of a loved one or as a gift to the church, and is being formally dedicated during a time of worship, then the relevant prayer can be prefaced by the following:

We come today to dedicate this gift *[or name of item]*,
  in loving memory of *[Name of donor or of deceased]*.
Let us consecrate it now to God's service,
  in warm appreciation,
  sincere respect,
  and heartfelt thanksgiving.

96
Consecration of a cross

Lord Jesus Christ,
  speak through this cross of love—
  your readiness to suffer and die
  so that we might have life in all its fullness.
Speak of humility—
  the way you willingly surrendered everything,
  emptying yourself and taking the form of a servant,
  our interests placed before your own.
Speak of victory—
  your triumph over evil, hatred, and death,
  over whatever frustrates your purpose
  or denies your goodness.
Speak of grace—
  your offer of free and total forgiveness,
  not because we deserve it
  but because, despite our repeated faults and failures,
  your nature is always to have mercy.

Speak of hope—
>the new beginnings you daily make possible,
>the fresh start that is always open to us,
>the promise that you are with us always
>holding unimagined blessing yet in store.

Bless, then, this cross,
>that it may speak of you,
>and grant that all it symbolizes
>might be reflected in our life together,
>our work and witness,
>to the glory of your name.

Amen.

97
Consecration of an organ/piano/keyboard

Loving God,
>celebrating once more the gift of music,
>and recognizing anew the way it is able to move, uplift,
>enthral, and inspire us,
>speaking both *of* you and *for* you,
>so now we consecrate this instrument to your service,
>with heartfelt praise and glad thanksgiving.

May it help us to lift up our hearts and voices,
>and to express our faith and worship,
>joy and gratitude,
>love and commitment—
>our music and song echoed by the discipleship we offer,
>to the glory of your name.

Amen.

98
Consecration of chairs/pews

Almighty God,
>we consecrate this new seating to you,
grateful for the opportunity,
week by week,
to gather here and worship,
to sit quietly,
and to hear both the reading and proclamation
of your word.

May these *chairs/pews* be to us also
>a symbol of the fellowship we share
with those past, present, and future—
those who have gathered here before us,
those we worship with now,
and those who will take our place in times to come—
and may that inspire us faithfully to play our part
as members of the great company of your people,
called together through Jesus Christ our Lord.

Amen.

99
Consecration of a stained-glass window

Sovereign God,
>may this window not only move us by its unique beauty
but speak similarly of the vibrancy, joy, and wonder
you have brought through Christ into our lives.

May the light that shines through it
>be echoed by the light of Christ shining in our hearts.

And, just as light will shine *out* as well as *in*,
>grant that the radiance of Christ
may shine from our hearts,
the splendor and wonder of his presence

reflected in our love for you,
  for one another,
  and for all.
In his name we pray.
Amen.

100
Consecration of a memorial plaque

God of past, present, and future,
  we erect this plaque in grateful memory of *[Name]*,
  recognizing all we owe to *his/her* work among us.
May this plaque offer a small but powerful reminder
  of everything *[Name]* has done among us,
  and of the immeasurable contribution *he/she* has made
  to our life together.
Above all,
  help us to honor *him/her*,
  not simply through this outward sign of remembrance,
  but also through displaying similar commitment,
  showing the same faith
  and offering equal service.
Grant, then, that not just a name
  but everything that name embodied
  will continue to live on through our life and witness,
  to the glory of Christ our savior.
Amen.

101
Consecration of an altar/communion table

Mighty and mysterious God,
   through this *altar/table*
   speak to us of your living presence,
   your saving love,
   your supreme sacrifice,
   and your amazing grace.
Remind us,
   through the breaking of bread and pouring out of wine—
   our sharing together in the body and blood of Christ—
   that you delight in our worship,
   gladly welcoming us as your people,
   your purpose never defeated,
   your mercy inexhaustible,
   and your goodness unfailing.
In that faith,
   and symbolizing that assurance,
   we consecrate this *altar/table* now,
   in the name of Christ.
Amen.

102
Consecration of a banner

Creator God,
   through the painstaking work
   that has crafted this banner,
   speak of the way you formed the universe,
   created our world,
   and fashioned our lives.
Through all this banner depicts,
   remind us of your living word,
   your involvement in history,
   your eternal purpose,
   and your saving love revealed in Christ.

Through the color, artistry, and symbolism
   of this banner,
   guide our thoughts in worship,
   aiding our meditation
   and drawing us closer to you,
   in Jesus's name.
Amen.

103
Consecration of kneelers

Servant God,
   for these kneelers—
   often unnoticed despite the dedication
   that has gone into creating them,
   taken for granted,
   without even a second glance,
   yet enabling us to kneel in your presence
   and draw closer to you in prayer and worship—
   we thank you.
Teach us, in turn,
   to be used in whatever way you see fit,
   without any thought of reward or recognition,
   but glad simply to serve
   and in some way to bring honor and glory to you,
   through Jesus Christ our Lord.
Amen.

104
Consecration of a font

Lord Jesus Christ,
    we consecrate this font to you,
    asking that you will bless in turn
    all those brought here for baptism,
    encircling them in your arms,
    embracing them in your love,
    enfolding them in your grace.
Speak here of the way you welcomed children to your side
    and of the childlike qualities you yearn to see in us all:
    the trust, innocence,
    eagerness, and openness
    that will mark out those
    who inherit the kingdom of heaven.
So may this font be a symbol to us and to all
    of your call to faith,
    your gift of mercy,
    and your promise of new life.
Amen.

105
Consecration of a baptismal pool

Gracious God,
    we commit to you not just this baptistry,
    but also and especially all those
    who will pass through it,
    confessing their faith in you,
    and testifying to the new beginnings,
    the joy, hope, love, and peace,
    you have brought into their lives.

May this pool,
   and their witness,
   be a constant reminder of your saving grace,
   your transforming power,
   and your daily call to be your people,
   redeemed, restored, and renewed in Christ.
Amen.

106
Consecration of a chalice

Lord Jesus Christ,
   may this chalice be to us
   an unforgettable symbol of your immense love,
   calling us to remember,
   each time we see it,
   the extent of your commitment,
   both to your Father's will and to our eternal welfare.
Help us to grasp again,
   whenever we drink,
   the awesome wonder of our redemption,
   the astonishing depth of your devotion,
   the stark reality of your sacrifice,
   and the incomparable richness of your gift—
   life now and always.
Through the cup lifted up
   and wine poured out and shared,
   may we remember, receive, and rejoice.
Amen.

107
Consecration of a communion plate

Lord Jesus Christ,
 just as this plate is incomplete without bread,
 so something is missing from our lives without you.
Remind us, whenever we gather, of that truth,
 and, each time bread is broken and shared,
 remind us also that
 through the new life you offer,
 won by your dying and rising again,
 your surrendering of all
 so that we might receive grace upon grace,
 you have met that need
 and answered our emptiness.
So, then, we ask,
 bless all that we offer to you now—
 this plate,
 our worship and sacrament,
 our discipleship,
 our lives—
 and use it to your glory.
Amen.

108
Consecration of facilities for the disabled

Sovereign God,
 celebrating the way you welcome us into your presence,
 overcoming every obstacle
 and breaking down the barriers that keep us apart,
 so we consecrate these new facilities to you,
 created to ensure that,
 as far as possible,
 no physical disability prevents people from worshiping
 here among us.

Remind us, today and always, of the needs of all,
    and teach us, each day,
    sensitively, compassionately, and lovingly,
    to open our hearts to each other
    as you have opened your all to us.
Amen.

109
Consecration of bells/bell-ropes

Lord of the Church,
Lord of the world,
    we consecrate these *bells/bell-ropes* to you,
    installed so that, as in times gone by,
    so in the years to come,
    they might ring out in your name
    and resound to your glory.
Grant that they may speak of you
    and of the fellowship we share in this place;
    that they may peal in celebration
    and toll in solemn remembrance;
    that they may uplift, inspire, challenge, and beckon,
    summoning to prayer and calling to worship.
As they ring out week by week,
    may they remind us of your call to reach out likewise
    and to make you known, in word and deed,
    through Jesus Christ our Lord.
Amen.

110
Consecration of a church notice board

Gracious God,
   help us through this board
   to make known the life and activities of this church—
   the worship we will offer,
   the fellowship share,
   the events stage
   and the programs organize—
   but help us to do so not for our own benefit or glory
   but to speak simply of you
   and of everything you want to do in this community,
   to communicate something of the gospel,
   and to make known, as best we can,
   your love and concern for all.
So may those who pass by be drawn in among us,
   hear your word,
   and come to know for themselves the faith we proclaim
   and the hope we share.
Amen.

111
Consecration of a church Bible

Almighty God,
   we consecrate this Bible to you,
   not as decoration or part of the furnishings
   but as a constant reminder of your living word,
   spoken across the centuries,
   recorded in Scripture and made flesh in Christ—
   a word that challenges and rebukes,
   comforts and strengthens,
   nurtures and nourishes,
   enthrals and inspires—
   your word that leads to life.

May it be, then,
- a symbol,
- a source of truth,
- and a call to action,
- inspiring us to read, listen, study, and seek,
- so that as you have spoken of old,
- so you will also speak now to us,
- this and every day.

Amen.

112
Consecration of hymn books

Great and glorious God,
- in response to your great goodness and faithfulness
- we delight to lift up our hearts and voices to you
- in glad thanksgiving and joyful praise.

So now we consecrate these hymn books to you,
- asking that through them you will help us
- to sing songs both old and new,
- expressing our faith,
- gratitude,
- love,
- awe,
- repentance,
- intercession,
- togetherness,
- and celebration.

May the resource they offer enable us
- to add our voice to the choir of angels,
- the heavenly host,
- the chorus of adoration that acclaims and adores
- your holy name,
- now and for all eternity.

Amen.

113
Consecration of prayer books

Sovereign God,
>   we commit these books to you,
>   asking that they will speak not just *of* you
>   but also *to* you,
>   helping us to express
>   something of our love and gratitude,
>   remorse and repentance,
>   faith and commitment—
>   our desire to live as your people
>   and to serve you more faithfully.

As we share over the months and years ahead
>   in prayer and response,
>   help us to make the words we use our own,
>   believing in our heart what we declare with our lips,
>   and offering living worship,
>   in Spirit and in truth,
>   through Jesus Christ our Lord.

Amen.

114
Consecration of a church library

Lord of all,
>   in humility we consecrate this library to you,
>   conscious that,
>   however much we may have understood of your love
>   and discerned of your purpose,
>   you have far more to reveal,
>   our knowledge for now at best
>   like looking through frosted glass—
>   partial and incomplete.

Use, then, the books collected here
   to open our hearts to new insights,
   deeper truths,
   and a fuller appreciation of who and what you are.
Stretch, challenge, rebuke, and prompt us,
   and so teach us to love and serve you better,
   through Jesus Christ our Lord.
Amen.

115
Consecration of an amplification/public address system

God of all,
   we consecrate this amplification system to you,
   eager that as many as possible may hear your word here
   and share together in the worship we offer,
   fully able to participate, listen, and respond.
We come, though, conscious that,
   when it comes to your voice,
   our hearing can be as impaired as any;
   that though we may have ears to hear,
   we do not always want to listen
   or take in what you are saying,
   our minds closed to awkward truths
   we would rather not face.
Help us, then,
   as we worship week by week,
   to open our hearts and souls to you,
   to hear what you are saying
   and to respond,
   through Jesus Christ our Lord.
Amen.

116
Consecration of an audio-visual system

Sovereign God,
    receive this system that we present today,
    and through it help us to worship you
    not just with our minds,
    through words,
    but with our hearts, eyes, and ears,
    through music and pictures,
    rejoicing in the world of sight and sound,
    the awesome wonder and variety of all we see and hear.
Show us how to use these media wisely and reverently,
    not as a gimmick or latest fad
    but as a tool in focusing more fully on your presence,
    in learning more of you
    and in celebrating all you have done and given.
In Christ's name we pray.
Amen.

117
Consecration of a church clock

Everlasting God,
    faithful and true,
    the same yesterday, today, and tomorrow,
    remind us, as we commit this clock to you,
    of your unchanging purpose,
    constant love,
    dependable goodness,
    and inexhaustible grace.
Remind us that,
    though the years slip past,
    though generations come and go

and empires rise and fall,
always you will be with us,
on earth and in heaven,
by our sides now and for all eternity—
one God,
world without end.
Amen.

118
Consecration of a church passenger vehicle

For this vehicle, and all it makes possible,
    God, we thank you.
Sanctify it by your grace,
    that it might provide long and valued service,
    both for us and the wider community.
Watch over all who travel in it—
    the infirm and disabled,
    young people and youth organizations,
    school and college groups—
    granting a safe journey and good fellowship,
    and bless equally those who drive it,
    giving them patience, attentiveness,
    and proficiency on the road.
Be there always,
    to guide and protect,
    a constant companion along the way,
    through Jesus Christ our Lord.
Amen.

Church Events

119
Blessing of a multi-church event

Lord of the Church,
Lord of all,
   we consecrate this time to you,
   asking that, by your grace,
   it might be more than a cosmetic exercise,
   a superficial display of unity,
   more pretence than reality.
Break down barriers of fear and suspicion,
   hesitation and reserve,
   so that there may be a true meeting together,
   a building of relationships,
   an establishment of trust and dialogue,
   and, above all, not only an awareness
   of our common humanity
   but also a recognition of the faith
   that unites us in Christ.
Draw us together now,
   so that in time we may grow and work together
   as your people,
   to your glory.
Amen.

120
Blessing of an interfaith project/event

Mighty and mysterious God,
   grant your blessing on this *project/event*,
   so that, recognizing our differences
   of faith, tradition, and conviction,
   we may nonetheless work together,
   recognizing also our common humanity,

    our mutual sincerity,
    our desire to build bridges,
    heal wounds,
    respect insights,
    and establish meaningful relationships.
Come, then,
    and, whatever we conceive you to be,
    may we sense your presence among us
    and in each other.
Amen.

121
Blessing of a public expression of faith

Lord Jesus Christ,
    we commit this march to you,
    not as a triumphalist procession
    or an attempt to impose our beliefs on others,
    still less to parade our faith or virtue in public,
    but simply and sincerely to point to you
    and to the fact that you still change lives,
    win hearts,
    and inspire commitment.
Though many will ignore us,
    others be puzzled,
    and a few perhaps even ridicule,
    grant that at least someone, somewhere,
    might be prompted to pause,
    consider,
    and explore further why we walk
    and whom we point to—
    seeds being sown that,
    in the fullness of time,
    might bear fruit for you.
Amen.

122
Blessing of an outreach service/event

Lord Jesus Christ,
> we cannot argue or persuade people into faith,
> nor would we want to.

We cannot win their hearts and minds by our own efforts,
> however skilled our methods
> or slick our presentation.

It needs your grace,
> your love,
> your Spirit to work within individuals' lives,
> prompting,
> stirring,
> challenging,
> and renewing.

So we ask your blessing on this venture,
> asking you to guide all we do, say, and think,
> and to work through it,
> in your own way and time,
> to your glory and for your kingdom.

Amen.

123
Blessing of a harvest supper

Sovereign God,
> as we eat together,
> speak through all that we will share.

Remind us of the intricate web of life
> and our responsibility
> to honor and respect your creation.

Remind us of the complex web of trade
> and our calling to work for justice.

Remind us of the web of production
> and our indebtedness to all who labor,
> in a multitude of ways,
> to provide the food we so easily take for granted.

Sanctify this meal,
> so that we might recognize more fully,
> and give thanks more frequently,
> for all we owe to you
> and to others.

Amen.

124
Blessing of a church meal/event to fight hunger

Lord,
> we are fortunate never to know real hunger,
> never to suffer the effects of malnutrition,
> never to experience the anguish
> of watching loved ones suffer and die
> through starvation;
> nor, through a simple meal such as this,
> can we ever begin to emphasize,
> still less identify with them.

But what we *can* do is recognize how lucky we are,
> consider the plight of others,
> and, through denying ourselves,
> give more generously to others.

Hallow, then, this meal,
> that the money we raise might help bring relief
> to those who truly hunger,
> and that—
> capturing our imagination,
> quickening our conscience,
> and stirring our vision—
> it may prompt us more often to have a little less
> so that others may have so much more.

Amen.

125
Blessing of a church lunch

Gracious God,
    through this time of eating together,
    nourish not just our bodies but our fellowship,
    our life together as your people.
Bless us through our talking and listening,
    our serving and being served,
    our preparing and clearing away,
    our enjoyment of good food and company.
Grant us, through it all,
    a sense of the joy and privilege of being your people,
    the fulfillment of belonging,
    the enrichment of giving and receiving
    in your name,
    and so may we grow closer to you
    and to one another,
    through Jesus Christ our Lord.
Amen.

126
Blessing of a church fundraiser

God of joy and blessing,
    we commit this charity fundraiser to you,
    asking that all the work that has made it possible—
    the planning and organizing,
    preparing and setting up,
    staffing and collecting—
    will bear fruit today.
Though our aim is to raise funds,
    may that not be our sole or chief objective,
    our concern, rather, being to provide pleasure,
    to promote enjoyment,
    to share fun, laughter, and camaraderie
    with those who attend.

Grant that in seeing the human face of our fellowship,
    some perhaps might consider the one behind it,
    and catch, in their own way, a glimpse of you.
Amen.

127
Blessing of a craft exhibit

Loving God,
    speak through the items displayed here
    of both human creativity
    and your own—
    of the ability you have given us
    to fashion, shape, craft, and mold;
    of the way you in turn have made all,
    forming life out of dust,
    bringing order out of chaos,
    everything that is, has been, and shall be,
    brought into being by your mighty hand.
Bless, then, this exhibit,
    that it may testify to the gifts you have given
    and the way they can be used to your glory.
Amen.

128
Blessing of a flower festival

Living God,
>   sanctify this festival
>   and all the painstaking, loving work that lies behind it,
>   for we offer it not just as a display of flowers,
>   special though they are,
>   but as a celebration of the beauty that surrounds us,
>   an expression of our awe and wonder,
>   a witness to your creative power
>   and a response to your faithful provision.

Through this tapestry of color, form,
>   texture, and fragrance,
>   and the way each has been woven together,
>   stir the hearts of all who enter here,
>   breathing something of your peace into their soul
>   and causing them to glimpse you more fully,
>   both here and in this wonderful world you have given.

In Christ's name we pray.
Amen.

129
Blessing of a church concert

(*delete from or add to as appropriate)

We come, Lord, today,
>   not to offer technical perfection or professional mastery,
>   but simply to celebrate your gifts of music, song,
>   drama, and poetry*—
>   to appreciate,
>   acknowledge,
>   and encourage,
>   recognizing the skills among us,
>   the work involved in developing them,
>   and the pleasure they can afford.

Help those who will lead and entertain us
    to give of their best,
    and to enjoy participating
    as much as we enjoy watching and listening.
So, send us on our way afterward,
    with music in our hearts
    and a new song on our lips,
    to the glory of your name.
Amen.

130
Blessing of a youth group event

Gracious God,
    we commit this holiday club to you,
    seeking not to indoctrinate or impose beliefs,
    nor to take advantage
    of young and impressionable lives,
    but simply to give children of this neighborhood
    the opportunity to hear of you,
    so that in due course,
    in their own way and time,
    they might consider the claims of the gospel
    for themselves,
    and be able to make an informed decision
    concerning their response.
Grant, then, your blessing
    on all involved in staging this venture
    and all who will share in it,
    in Jesus's name.
Amen.

131
Blessing of a quiet day or retreat

Sanctify this time and space, Lord,
    and help us in turn to make time and space for you,
    setting aside room in our lives to be still
    and know that you are God;
    to draw aside from the bustle of this world
    and to reflect,
    emptying our minds and opening our hearts
    that we might unlock a window
    through which to glimpse you more fully
    and respond more freely.
Meet with us here,
    that we may meet you everywhere,
    in all we do,
    and all we meet,
    through Jesus Christ our Lord.
Amen.

132
Blessing of a church anniversary

Through the rich history of this church—
    the faith, example, and legacy of past generations—
    grant your blessing, O Lord.
Through one another here today—
    the inspiration, encouragement,
    joy, and support found in worship and fellowship—
    grant your blessing, O Lord.
Through all the future holds—
    plans made,
    initiatives started,
    goals achieved—
    grant your blessing, O Lord.

Speak, through these celebrations,
  of all you have done,
  are doing,
  and will yet do,
  and in it all
  grant your blessing, O Lord.
Amen.

133
Blessing of a church outing

Bless this day, Lord, and all it will bring.
In the journey we will make,
  company enjoy,
  conversations hold,
  sights see,
  and fun share,
  may friendships be cemented,
  relationships enriched,
  and fellowship deepened.
Through being, laughing, and unwinding together,
  may we also *grow* together,
  united more firmly as a family of your people,
  through Jesus Christ our Lord.
Amen.

134
Blessing of a church weekend

Gracious God,
    touch this time together
    through your loving and living presence,
    so that it may be a time of fun, refreshment,
    and growing together—
    a time in which we learn more both of you
    and of one another.
Grant that through being here
    and all we will share together,
    love will grow between us:
    trust,
    understanding,
    mutual concern,
    friendships being cemented,
    and new relationships established.
Draw us together in faith, vision, and fellowship,
    and so help us to grow as your people,
    your children—
    a family in Christ.
Amen.

135
Blessing of a church/council meeting

Gracious God,
    grant your blessing on this time together,
    that it may be not merely a meeting
    but, above all, a meeting together—
    with you
    and one another—
    a meeting of minds as we listen,
    share,
    reflect,
    discuss,
    seeking more clearly to discern your will
    and honor your purpose.

Grant us wisdom, humility,
> vision, and faith,
> that your love may guide our deliberations,
> inform our decisions,
> enrich our fellowship,
> and inspire our service,
> each offered to you through Jesus Christ our Lord.
Amen.

136
Blessing of a new house group/study group

Living Lord,
> we consecrate this meeting,
> and each one of us here,
> to you,
> asking you to speak through all we share:
> the words we read,
> thoughts contribute,
> questions discuss,
> and prayers offer;
> the ideas we consider,
> truths explore,
> and insights gain;
> the fellowship we enjoy,
> friendships strengthen,
> and trust foster as a result.

Bless every aspect of our being here,
> and our being together,
> that we may grow together
> in faith, love, vision, and service,
> to the glory of your name.
Amen.

The Lord's Supper

137
Blessing of bread (1)

In broken bread, Lord,
   be present,
   and touch our lives.
Nourish, refresh,
   fill, and bless
   in body, mind, and soul.
Amen.

138
Blessing of bread (2)

Gracious God,
   sanctify this bread,
   so that,
   nourished in spirit and renewed in faith,
   we may know you more fully,
   love you more deeply,
   trust you more strongly,
   and serve you more truly,
   through Jesus Christ our Lord.
Amen.

139
Blessing of bread (3)

Bless this bread, Lord of life,
    and speak through it of grace,
    sacrifice,
    love,
    and new beginnings—
    the price you paid
    and victory won,
    for us
    and for all.
Amen.

140
Blessing of bread (4)

Through Christ broken
    may we be made whole
Through bread broken
    may we be filled.
Through this sacred moment
    may God sanctify our worship
    and consecrate our lives
    to his glory.
Amen.

141
Blessing of wine (1)

Father God,
   take this cup,
   and through your poured-out blood
   transform the water of our lives into wine.
Revive,
   restore,
   refresh,
   renew,
   through Jesus Christ our Lord.
Amen.

142
Blessing of wine (2)

In wine poured out for you
   and blood shed for many
   may God quench your thirst
   and refresh your spirit.
May he satisfy your deepest need,
   filling you with joy, hope, peace, and love,
   this day and forevermore.
Amen.

143
Blessing of wine (3)

Take our thirst, Lord,
   and meet it.
Take our worship
   and bless it.
Take our faith
   and increase it.
Take our service
   and use it.
Take what we are
   and direct what we shall be,
   by your grace.
Amen.

144
Blessing of wine (4)

The new wine of Christ course within you,
   filling your heart,
   flooding your soul,
   and flowing from your life,
   to his glory.
Amen.

Money

145
Blessing of a weekly offering (1)

Through this money, Lord,
   we offer our worship,
   our thanks,
   our love,
   and our praise.
Bless it all,
   and touch it by your grace,
   so that what we give,
   what we do,
   and what we are
   may bring glory to you.
Amen.

146
Blessing of a weekly offering (2)

Generous and loving God,
   we give this money to you,
   not dutifully but joyfully,
   not grudgingly but thankfully,
   not because we must but because we may—
   an offering instead of a collection,
   given from the heart,
   with gratitude,
   love,
   and praise.
Receive it,
   and use it as you will,
   in your service
   for Christ's sake.
Amen.

147
Blessing of a weekly offering (3)

Gracious God,
    poor though it is,
    take what we offer
    and use it in ways beyond our imagining
    to promote your kingdom and make known your love.
Weak though *we* are,
    take us in turn,
    and use us how and where you will
    to further your will and make known your grace.
Accept our flawed and hesitant response,
    and, by your grace, work through it,
    to your glory.
Amen.

148
Blessing of a weekly offering (4)

Take this money, Lord,
    and *provide* through it.
Take our faith
    and *work* through it.
Take our love
    and *minister* through it.
Take our witness
    and *speak* through it.
Receive these gifts as a sign of all we would offer,
    in grateful response
    and joyful service,
    through Jesus Christ our Lord.
Amen.

149
Blessing of a weekly offering (5)

Loving God,
   bless this money and those who give it,
   that all may be sanctified by your touch
   and used to your glory,
   through Jesus Christ our Lord.
Amen.

150
Consecration of a collection for charity

As you have blessed us, Lord,
   use this money to bless others.
We offer it in love,
   conscious of all we have received,
   and eager to show our gratitude,
   not just through words,
   but through helping in some small way
   to make a difference.
Take it, we ask,
   and, by your grace, may it bring help and hope,
   health and happiness,
   new beginnings—
   the possibility of real and lasting change.
In Christ's name we pray.
Amen.

151
Consecration of proceeds from a fundraising event

Gracious God,
  we consecrate this money to you,
  conscious of all the time and effort
  that has gone into raising it,
  truly grateful for the dedication—
  to you, this church, and others—
  that it represents.
Help us to use it prudently,
  generously,
  prayerfully,
  and lovingly,
  so that the use to which it is put
  may recognize and honor that commitment,
  and in a real, if small, way express your love
  and further your kingdom,
  through Jesus Christ our Lord.
Amen.

152
Consecration of a gift

For the generosity that has inspired this gift,
  and the one who has given it,
  Lord, we praise you.
Bless whatever it is used for,
  so that we will show our gratitude
  not just through words,
  but also through faithful stewardship,
  using it, in the spirit it was given,
  for others as well as ourselves,
  and, above all, for you
  and to your glory.
Amen.

153
Consecration of a legacy

Sovereign God,
> for this bequest and all it makes possible,
> we thank you,
> remembering *[Name of donor]* with gratitude
> and resolved to use *her/his* gift wisely and faithfully.

We commit it, then, to your service,
> asking for guidance in how best to employ it,
> so that, whether invested or spent,
> financing existing work or funding new projects,
> benefiting us or others,
> the result may be a fitting tribute to *[Name of donor]*,
> a lasting legacy,
> honoring both *her/him* and you.

Amen.

Places

154
Consecration/re-consecration of a cemetery/graveyard

Be present in this *cemetery/graveyard*, Lord,
   and fill it with your peace.
May it be honored by all as a final resting place,
   hallowed ground,
   sanctified by the tears of loss,
   the anguish of separation,
   the bittersweet pain of remembrance,
   and, amid the shock and sorrow,
   the heartache and numbness,
   the fond farewells,
   grant here your peace that passes understanding,
   comfort in the shadow of death,
   and the promise of continuing life,
   now and for all eternity,
   through Jesus Christ our Lord.
Amen.

155
Consecration/re-consecration of a crematorium

Gracious God,
    we consecrate this crematorium
    and all who work here to you,
    asking that, through the service offered,
    you will reach out to the bereaved and broken,
    giving them the chance,
    reverently and lovingly,
    to commit their loved ones to you
    with the dignity and respect they deserve.
Here, in the valley of tears,
    may they also find peace,
    comfort,
    compassion,
    and hope—
    a place to grieve but also give thanks,
    to let go but also remember,
    to come to terms with death
    and find assurance of life to come,
    through Jesus Christ our Lord.
Amen.

156
Dedication of a garden of remembrance

Be present, Lord, in this place of tranquillity,
    and through its quiet beauty
        breathe peace into the hearts of those who grieve here,
        fondly remembering lost loved ones.
May the cycle of the seasons that unfolds in this garden
    speak of your continuing faithfulness
    and your bringing of life out of death,
    beginnings out of endings.

So may memories be touched with anticipation,
    sorrow with gratitude,
    despair with hope,
    and tears with laughter,
    life beckoning once more with fresh promise,
    both for now and all eternity.
Amen.

157
Dedication of a tree planted in memory of a loved one

Sovereign God,
    just as one dearly loved will live on in our hearts,
    the memories bringing joy and gratitude,
    celebration of so much shared,
    so may this tree live on for generations to come—
    a visible sign of love,
    a symbol of thankfulness,
    an expression of untold happiness, given and received.
May it stand as a memorial that brings joy to others
    and enrichment to the landscape,
    and may both the life within it
    and the life it supports
    speak of your life-giving power,
    your renewing and energizing love,
    through which we and all your people
    will rise again to new life,
    in your eternal kingdom,
    through Jesus Christ our Lord.
Amen.

Animals

158
Blessing of a new family pet

Lord of all,
    we thank you for *[Name of pet]*
    and for the excitement *her/his* coming has caused.
Watch over *her/him*,
    protecting from accident or illness
    and granting a long and full life,
    that *s/he* may bring joy,
    enrichment,
    companionship,
    and affection—
    and that we, in turn,
    may offer the care, dedication,
    nourishment, and nurture *s/he* needs
    for health and happiness,
    vigor and contentment.
Amen.

159
Blessing when a pet has to be put down

Loving God,
    in the anguish of this moment,
    faced with losing not just a pet but a companion—
    one who has been part of life,
    bringing so much happiness,
    inspiring such affection,
    and sharing so many special moments—
    give courage to make the right decision,
    and blessing in doing so.
Though loss will be painful,
    may it willingly be borne to save *[Name]*
    the bewilderment of inexorable decline,
    and the suffering this would inevitably involve,
    and may that thought give strength now
    and comfort in days to come.
Amen.

160
Blessing at the burial of a family pet

Loving Lord,
    with thanks for everything *[Name]* has meant to us—
    the delight given,
    the fun shared,
    the happiness afforded,
    the love inspired—
    gratefully we say goodbye,
    celebrating the joy we have known,
    the innumerable ways that *[Name]* has brightened life,
    never to be forgotten.
Come now, as we commit *his/her* body to the ground,
    and grant us your comfort,
    today and in the days ahead.
Amen.

161
Blessing of an animal sanctuary

Be in this place of care and compassion, Lord,
   and minister through it to the creatures brought here,
   each the work of your hands,
   precious in your sight.
After the trauma so many have experienced,
   may they find relief here—
   instead of abuse, affection,
   instead of neglect, nurture,
   instead of rejection, love,
   instead of pain, pleasure.
May wounds be tended,
   disease treated,
   sickness stemmed,
   and injuries healed—
   your broken creation made whole,
   in Christ's name.
Amen.